Squealing Mad Pigs

by darren

Kevin Mayhew

First published in 1999 by
KEVIN MAYHEW LTD
Buxhall
Stowmarket
Suffolk IP14 3DJ

0 1 2 3 4 5 6 7 8 9

ISBN 1 84003 316 9
Catalogue No 1500244

Cover illustration by Darren
Edited by David Gatward
Printed and bound in Great Britain

You know that feeling you get when someone's telling you a long funny story or a joke and you're conscious that come the end some sort of visible display of humorous appreciation will be necessary, albeit sincere (which you hope you'll manage) or merely polite (which you're sure everybody notices)? Anyway, the point is it can be a slight worry sometimes wouldn't you say?

So imagine then that instead, you're proudly presented with an actual cartoon joke - by the artist himself (having spent all afternoon lovingly nursing it to full comic potential), who then watches for your response (whilst naturally pretending he isn't). To me that sounds less like a 'slight worry' and more like 'definite pressure'!

So this is a big thank you to those of you round here often enough to be faced with such 'laugh or die' situations — in particular, my skilfully supportive parents, happier than ever jeremy and rachael, Samber - the friendly footfalls on our ceiling and to my snub-nosed little love bomb - i think you're wonderful!

Although the rest of you go unmentioned you are all very much appreciated - thank you!

— x.

to monster
you make me happy
x

When Jesus entered Gerasa, he was met by a man filled with evil spirits. Jesus ordered the spirits out of the man and into a herd of pigs feeding on a hillside nearby. The herd promptly rushed down the hill into the lake and drowned.

Mark 5:11-13

WHERE AM I ?!
DON'T WORRY - I CAST THEM INTO THE PIGS, EVERYONE'S QUITE SAFE NOW
SQUEEE
SQUEEEEEE
SQUEEEE
SQUEEEEEEE
what's that noise...
OK class - five more minutes then we have to pack up

'Now the serpent was more crafty than any of the animal's the Lord God had made.'

Genesis 3:1

THERE WAS NO DOUBT AMONG THE ANIMALS OF EDEN THAT THE SERPENT WAS THE "MOST CRAFTY"

Surely I don't need to summarise this bit. Doesn't everybody know this story?

ONE TINY OVERSIGHT AND DINOSAURS BECAME EXTINCT

When Jesus visited Jericho
a short man named
Zacchaeus could not see him
for the crowds, so he
climbed a tree for a
better view.

Luke 19:1-4

AFTER ZACCHAEUS HAD BEEN UP THE TREE FOR THE BEST PART OF A DAY AND STILL NOT SEEN ANYTHING HE DECIDED HIS IDEA WOULD PROBABLY WORK BETTER IN THE AUTUMN

Delilah tried to deceive Samson into revealing the weakness behind his incredible strength, so she might betray him to the Philistines.

Samson told her that for him to be tied with seven bow strings was the answer, although it proved to be a lie. Then Samson told Delilah it was new ropes; also a lie. A rope made from his own hair – a lie. Get the picture?

Judges 16:1-14

DELILAH WAS STUPID AS WELL AS UNTRUSTWORTHY

Elijah challenged the prophets of Baal to prove their god's existence by calling on him to provide the fire for their prepared sacrifice. They danced and shouted all day long to no avail.

Elijah however, prayed a simple prayer to the Lord God and fire fell from heaven consuming his sacrifice.

1 Kings 18:22-38

NALAM'S BARBECUES USED TO BE THE TALK OF THE TOWN UNTIL ELIJAH MOVED IN NEXT DOOR

In the Philistine camp
there was a giant from
Gath named Goliath.

1 Samuel 17:4

AS A CHILD GOLIATH WAS FREQUENTLY EXCLUDED FROM THE ACTIVITIES OF HIS PEERS

Over 5000 people gathered to hear Jesus teach, but come evening only one boy had any food - five loaves and two fishes. Jesus took the food and blessed it, then his disciples distributed it amongst all the people.

Everybody ate and was satisfied and the disciples picked up twelve baskets of pieces left over.

Matthew 14:15-21

Now look here boy – I only packed you five loaves and two fishes – you'd better not have any leftovers!

Water flooded the
earth for 150 days.
Genesis 7:24

NOAH'S EXHIBITION OF 'LANDSCAPE PAINTINGS WHILST ON THE ARK' MEETS WITH A BAD RESPONSE

When Joseph was working in Potiphar's household, his master's wife 'took notice' of him and attempted to seduce him. Joseph however, refused her advances.

Genesis 39 : 7-10

RESISTING POTIPHAR'S WIFE WASN'T ACTUALLY ALL THAT DIFFICULT

I'm not going to get myself into trouble here by even attempting to anchor this idea to anything Jesus ever said or did! (He actually called them vipers anyway, not frogs.)

ALTHOUGH HE NEVER ACTUALLY DID IT, THE IDEA ALWAYS BROUGHT A SMILE TO JESUS' LIPS

God made the wild animals according to their kinds, and when it was done He was pleased with what He saw.

Genesis 1 : 25

CREATING ANIMALS
1: GOD CREATES THE SPIDER

God worked several miracles in front of Pharaoh through Moses so that Pharaoh might be persuaded to free God's people, the Israelites. Pharaoh however, refused to be moved.

Exodus 7:8-13

IT WAS- BUT PHARAOH STILL WOULDN'T LET THE ISRAELITES GO

God confused the languages of man causing the tower they intended to build reaching into the heavens to remain unfinished.

Genesis 11 : 3-8

WHAT BECAME OF THE TOWER OF BABEL

In his pursuit of David, Saul 'relieved himself' in a cave that, unbeknown to him, David was hiding in. David intended Saul no harm and to prove this to the King, he cut a piece out of Saul's cloak and as Saul was leaving, David shouted out to him.

1 Samuel 24 : 3-10

DAVID LABOURS THE POINT

When Jesus visited Jericho
a short man named Zacchaeus
could not see him for the
crowds, so he climbed a
tree for a better view.

Luke 19:1-4

ZACCHAEUS SOON DISCOVERED HIS ATTENTION GRABBING ANTICS WERE JUST AS EFFECTIVE AT SOCIAL DINNERS AND PARTIES

The serpent came to the woman, tempting her to eat the forbidden fruit of the tree of good and evil.

Genesis 3:1-6

LOOK! I DON'T CARE WHAT YOU PREFER! IT'S AN APPLE TREE! THERE AREN'T ANY FLAMING BANANAS!
© d96

God sent Jonah to Nineveh but Jonah ran away from God (duh!) and took a boat to Tarshish. God sent a dreadful storm against the boat forcing the sailors to throw all the cargo overboard. Eventually, Jonah himself was thrown overboard and swallowed by a great fish God provided.

Jonah 1: 3-17

INSIDE THE WHALE JONAH'S SUSPICIONS ARE CONFIRMED

The disciples saw Jesus walking towards them on the surface of the water. Peter called out to Jesus who bade him 'come', so Peter too, walked on the water.

Matthew 14:25-29

THE SEA OF TIBERIAS

Methuselah lived 969 years and then he died. (see opposite.)

Genesis 5:27

THE THOUGHT OF ALL THOSE CANDLES TO BLOW OUT FINALLY PROVED TOO MUCH FOR METHUSELAH

The Israelites grumbled to Moses about their lack of water, complaining they should never have left Egypt. God commanded Moses to speak to a rock and it would bring forth water for the people.

Numbers 20: 2-11

NATURALLY THE ISRAELITES HAD COMPLAINED ABOUT JUST WATER

Since they could not get the paralysed man to Jesus because of the crowd, his friends made a hole in the roof above Jesus and lowered him on his mat into the room. Jesus saw their faith and he healed the man.

Mark 2:4-5

Hey – this is the room Jesus is teaching in isn't it? We've got a sick bloke to lower in – where's Jesus?

Elijah went to the wilderness east of the Jordan and there the Lord sent the ravens to bring him bread and meat in the mornings and evenings.

1 Kings 17:1-6

WHILST THE BREAD AND MEAT THE RAVENS BROUGHT WAS VERY PLEASANT, ELIJAH SOON DISCOVERED SOMETHING EVEN TASTIER

Again Saul pursued David and again David had to prove to Saul his lack of harmful intent towards him. Whilst Saul slept, David crept into the camp and stole the spear and water jug from beside Saul's head.

1 Samuel 26:7-12

MEN! DAVID WAS IN THE CAMP LAST NIGHT! HE'S TAKEN MY SPEAR, MY WATER JUG AND- .. why are you looking at me like that ?

So that Balaam's disob-
edience might be revealed,
the Lord opened his donkey's
mouth and enabled it to
speak.

Numbers 22:28

BALAAM WASN'T ONE TO MISS AN OPPORTUNITY

God created all the
wild animals according
to their kinds.

Genesis 1:25

CREATING ANIMALS
2: REVIEWING THE DOG

The Lord provided a
great fish to swallow
Jonah and he was inside
the fish for three days
and three nights.

Jonah 1:17

...well we were playing Jonah and the whale and ...er.. we couldn't find a whale so we caught this fish see and, well.. Simon was.. er.. Simon was Jonah right...

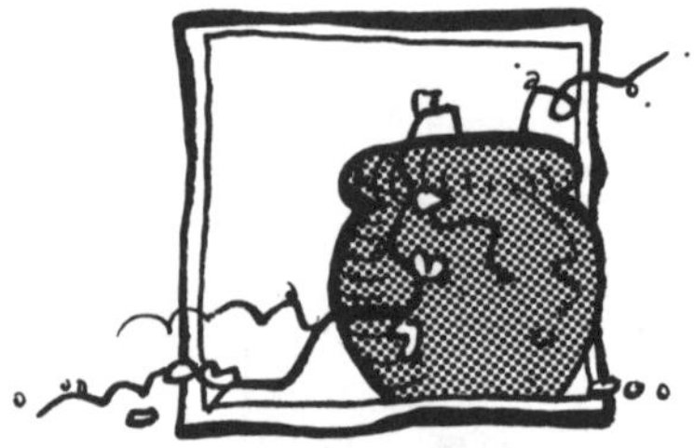

On his way to the city,
Jesus became hungry. Seeing
a fig tree by the side of
the road he went to look
for fruit but found nothing
except bare leaves. 'May
you never bear fruit again,'
Jesus said to it and
immediately the tree wilted
and died.

Matthew 21:18-19

THE NAZARENE GARDENERS' CLUB WAS REGRETTING THEIR CHOICE IN ASKING JESUS TO JUDGE THE ANNUAL VILLAGE COMPETITION

God provided Manna
for the Israelites to eat
during the forty years
they spent in the wilderness.

Exodus 16:14-20

ISRAEL'S WILDERNESS YEARS WERE NOT GOOD TIMES FOR EATING OUT

God told Noah to take a male and female of every animal on board the ark to keep their various kinds alive.

Genesis 7:1-4

Sorry Rover - the Lord was quite 'specific about who could come in the ark. Due to your little 'operation' i'm afraid you're going to have to stay here and drown

NOAH'S DOG

Jesus sent Peter to catch a fish from the lake. In its mouth he would find a four-drachma coin which he was to pay their taxes with.

Matthew 17:27

THE COMEDY POTENTIAL IN HIS EARLIER MIRACLE OBVIOUSLY HADN'T ESCAPED JESUS' ATTENTION

En route to Damascus, Paul suddenly found himself blinded by bright lights and heard the voice of God calling out to him.

Acts 9:3-4

OPERATION "DAMASCUS ROAD" WAS TURNING RAPIDLY PEAR-SHAPED

Jonathan set out to determine if Saul intended to kill David. He was to communicate his findings to David by a pre-arranged signal. Whilst David hid by the stone called 'Ezal', Jonathan would shoot an arrow to the side of it and send his errand boy to retrieve it. When the boy reached the arrow, Jonathan would shout, 'That's it! Bring it to me', for 'all clear', or, 'Isn't the arrow beyond you?' for 'danger.'

1 Samuel 20:18-22

"WAIT BY THE STONE CALLED 'EZEL' AND I'LL SHOOT AN ARROW TO THE SIDE OF IT" JONATHAN HAD TOLD DAVID. HE FORGOT TO SAY WHICH SIDE

Wise men came to the stable where Jesus was born, and they bowed down and worshipped him. Then they presented him with gifts of gold, frankincense, and myrrh.

Matthew 2:1-11

..AND WE BRING YOU GIFTS OF GOLD! FRANKINCENSE! .... and curd.
I THOUGHT THAT'S WHAT YOU SAID.

God brought all the animals to Adam who gave them their names. (OK, so it's not quite a party - I couldn't find that verse.)

Genesis 2:19-20

ADAM'S 'GET-TO-KNOW-THE-OTHER ANIMALS' PARTY WASN'T MUCH FUN FOR THE HERBIVORES

God appeared to Moses in a burning bush. When Moses approached, God ordered that he remove his sandals for the ground was holy.

Exodus 3:2-4

HAVING GROWN ACCUSTOMED TO THE WAYS OF THE DESERT, MOSES' PERSONAL HYGIENE WASN'T QUITE WHAT IT USED TO BE

Whilst in the desert the devil tempted Jesus for forty days.

Luke 4 : 1-2

FURTHER UNDOCUMENTED TEMPTATIONS OF JESUS

Jacob was cooking stew when Esau arrived starving from the open country. 'Let me have some of your stew,' he demanded from Jacob. 'Only if you give me your birthright in return,' Jacob replied. Esau agreed.

Genesis 25:29–34

HAVING JUST SECURED ESAU'S BIRTHRIGHT FOR A BOWL OF STEW, JACOB KNEW HE WAS ONTO SOMETHING

After the ark had come to rest, Noah sent out a dove to see if the bird would find dry ground.

Genesis 8:8

MRS NOAH PROVES TO BE SOMEWHAT MORE PRACTICAL THAN HER HUSBAND

God created all the
wild animals according
to their kinds.

Genesis 1:25

CREATING ANIMALS
3: CREATOR'S BLOCK

Jesus took his disciples to Bethany where he spoke to them for the last time before being taken up to heaven.

Luke 24:50-51

THE ASCENSION
(AND AN OPPORTUNITY JESUS JUST COULDN'T RESIST)

David killed the Philistine giant Goliath, as I'm sure you already know. Does anybody actually read these bits on the really well known stories? Maybe just a curious glance to see how I've managed to paraphrase such detailed and dramatic prose into one self-explanatory, two-inch sentence?

1 Samuel 17:48-50

THE NECESSARY FORMALITIES ARE OBSERVED IN THE PHILISTINE MORTUARY

The spirit of God came in power on Samson and he killed a lion with his bare hands. Some time later he passed the lion's carcass and found a swarm of bees and honey in it. Samson took some of the honey and ate it. He also gave some to his parents.

Judges 14:5-9

SAMSON'S GUESTS DIDN'T FEEL ALL THAT HUNGRY ANYMORE

Samuel was sleeping in the temple of the Lord when he heard a voice calling him. Believing it to be Eli, the temple priest Samuel went to him. Eli denied it and this happened three times before they realised it was God's voice Samuel was hearing.

1 Samuel 3:2-10

GOD'S MANNER OF SPEAKING TO SAMUEL THE PREVIOUS EVENING HAD GIVEN ELI AN IDEA

When Jesus entered Gerasa,
he was met by a man filled
with evil spirits. Jesus ordered
the spirits out of the man
and into a herd of pigs
feeding on a hillside nearby.
The herd promptly rushed
down the hill and into a
lake and drowned.

Mark 5:11-13

NOT EVERY SQUEALING MAD PIG DROWNED

ALSO AVAILABLE:

'Bible Dayze!'
(the first collection)

+

various cards, posters, knitwear & culinary items*

(* some of this is not true)